Welcome & Thank you

Congratulations

Self Care is important and you have taken a step forward by purchasing this workbook. I commend you for understanding how important your well being is. You have made yourself a priority. Doing so not only benefits you, but the people you love as well. The peopple who love you and depnd on you would much rather see you positive, full of energy and happy, than tired, unhappy and emotionally drainged.

This self care workbook will help to equip you with the knowledge and tools to make self care an ongoing part of your life's journey.

Thank you for choosing our workbook to assist you with your journey

Moreen Jordan, M.A., L.P.C.
Marital & Family Therapist

All rights reserved.
This publication is designed to provide information & enjoyment only.
It is sold with the understanding that the publisher and author is not engaged in rendering psychological, financial, legal or other professional services. Neither the publisher nor the author is engaged in rendering professional services or advice.
For more information contact moreenthetherapist@gmail.com

Copyright © 2018 by Moreen Jordan, M.A., L.P.C.
www.moreenjordan.com

The ideas, procedures, and suggestions contained in this book are not intended as a substitute for consulting with your physician or other health care provider. All matters regarding your health require medical supervision. Neither the author nor the publisher shall be liable for responsible for any loss or damages allegedly arising from any information or suggestion in this book.
If expert assistance or counseling is needed, the services of a competent professional should be sought. All handouts and worksheets can be photocopies for personal use with this program, but may not be reproduced for any other purpose without the written permission of the copyright owner.

Copyright @ 2022 by Moreen Jordan, M.A., L.P.C.
www.moreenjordan.com
ISBN; 978-1-7373521-8-1 (paperback)
Printed in the United States of American

First Edition 2022
First Printing 2022

Daily Gratitude Journal

I AM GRATFUL FOR	THE BEST THINGS ABOUT THIS WEEK

ISSUES I HAD AND WHAT CAN I DO TO MAKE IT BETTER

GOALS FOR NEXT WEEK	STEPS ACTION

THOUGHTS & REFLECTIONS

Moreen Jordan is a licensed mental health professional, Christian counselor, Speaker, Trainer and Consultant specializing in working with individuals, couples, families and corporations who have experienced trauma and/or witnessed traumatic events. She has worked with First responders and Military personnel both nationally and internationally. She is the President/CEO of Aspiring Life Change Counseling & Consulting, LLC And Compassion and Grace Counseling & Consulting (a non-profit organization).

Moreen empowers individuals and couples to overcome personal obstacles so that they can once again live purposeful and joy filled lives while honoring their past. Having overcome her own life-altering trauma, it has given her the passion to reach out to others and support them in their healing process. Moreen's own life is living proof of one's ability to overcome life's obstacles and she is determined to help others to reclaim their purpose, power and confidence.

She has her Master of Arts in Marital & Family Therapy and is a Licensed Professional Counselor. She is also a Certified Trauma Professional and Critical Incident Stress Debriefer (CISD) and has over 25+ years of counseling and behavioral health experience.

If you would like to contact her for a speaking engagement, training or other services please contact her at moreenthetherapist@gmail.com

Daily Gratitude Journal

I AM GRATEFUL FOR	THE BEST THINGS ABOUT THIS WEEK

ISSUES I HAD AND WHAT CAN I DO TO MAKE IT BETTER

GOALS FOR NEXT WEEK	STEPS ACTION

THOUGHTS & REFLECTIONS

Daily Gratitude Journal

I AM GRATFUL FOR	THE BEST THINGS ABOUT THIS WEEK

ISSUES I HAD AND WHAT CAN I DO TO MAKE IT BETTER

GOALS FOR NEXT WEEK	STEPS ACTION

THOUGHTS & REFLECTIONS

Daily Gratitude Journal

I AM GRATFUL FOR	THE BEST THINGS ABOUT THIS WEEK

ISSUES I HAD AND WHAT CAN I DO TO MAKE IT BETTER

GOALS FOR NEXT WEEK	STEPS ACTION

THOUGHTS & REFLECTIONS

Daily Gratitude Journal

I AM GRATFUL FOR	THE BEST THINGS ABOUT THIS WEEK

ISSUES I HAD AND WHAT CAN I DO TO MAKE IT BETTER

GOALS FOR NEXT WEEK	STEPS ACTION

THOUGHTS & REFLECTIONS

Daily Gratitude Journal

I AM GRATFUL FOR	THE BEST THINGS ABOUT THIS WEEK

ISSUES I HAD AND WHAT CAN I DO TO MAKE IT BETTER

GOALS FOR NEXT WEEK	STEPS ACTION

THOUGHTS & REFLECTIONS

Daily Gratitude Journal

I AM GRATFUL FOR	THE BEST THINGS ABOUT THIS WEEK

ISSUES I HAD AND WHAT CAN I DO TO MAKE IT BETTER

GOALS FOR NEXT WEEK	STEPS ACTION

THOUGHTS & REFLECTIONS

Daily Gratitude Journal

I AM GRATFUL FOR	THE BEST THINGS ABOUT THIS WEEK

ISSUES I HAD AND WHAT CAN I DO TO MAKE IT BETTER

GOALS FOR NEXT WEEK	STEPS ACTION

THOUGHTS & REFLECTIONS

Daily Gratitude Journal

I AM GRATFUL FOR	THE BEST THINGS ABOUT THIS WEEK

ISSUES I HAD AND WHAT CAN I DO TO MAKE IT BETTER

GOALS FOR NEXT WEEK	STEPS ACTION

THOUGHTS & REFLECTIONS

Daily Gratitude Journal

I AM GRATFUL FOR	THE BEST THINGS ABOUT THIS WEEK

ISSUES I HAD AND WHAT CAN I DO TO MAKE IT BETTER

GOALS FOR NEXT WEEK	STEPS ACTION

THOUGHTS & REFLECTIONS

Daily Gratitude Journal

I AM GRATFUL FOR	THE BEST THINGS ABOUT THIS WEEK

ISSUES I HAD AND WHAT CAN I DO TO MAKE IT BETTER

GOALS FOR NEXT WEEK	STEPS ACTION

THOUGHTS & REFLECTIONS

Daily Gratitude Journal

I AM GRATFUL FOR	THE BEST THINGS ABOUT THIS WEEK

ISSUES I HAD AND WHAT CAN I DO TO MAKE IT BETTER

GOALS FOR NEXT WEEK	STEPS ACTION

THOUGHTS & REFLECTIONS

Daily Gratitude Journal

I AM GRATFUL FOR	THE BEST THINGS ABOUT THIS WEEK

ISSUES I HAD AND WHAT CAN I DO TO MAKE IT BETTER

GOALS FOR NEXT WEEK	STEPS ACTION

THOUGHTS & REFLECTIONS

Daily Gratitude Journal

I AM GRATEFUL FOR	THE BEST THINGS ABOUT THIS WEEK

ISSUES I HAD AND WHAT CAN I DO TO MAKE IT BETTER

___

___

___

___

GOALS FOR NEXT WEEK	STEPS ACTION

THOUGHTS & REFLECTIONS

___

___

___

___

Daily Gratitude Journal

I AM GRATFUL FOR	THE BEST THINGS ABOUT THIS WEEK

ISSUES I HAD AND WHAT CAN I DO TO MAKE IT BETTER

GOALS FOR NEXT WEEK	STEPS ACTION

THOUGHTS & REFLECTIONS

Daily Gratitude Journal

I AM GRATFUL FOR	THE BEST THINGS ABOUT THIS WEEK

ISSUES I HAD AND WHAT CAN I DO TO MAKE IT BETTER

GOALS FOR NEXT WEEK	STEPS ACTION

THOUGHTS & REFLECTIONS

Daily Gratitude Journal

I AM GRATFUL FOR	THE BEST THINGS ABOUT THIS WEEK

ISSUES I HAD AND WHAT CAN I DO TO MAKE IT BETTER

GOALS FOR NEXT WEEK	STEPS ACTION

THOUGHTS & REFLECTIONS

Daily Gratitude Journal

I AM GRATFUL FOR	THE BEST THINGS ABOUT THIS WEEK

ISSUES I HAD AND WHAT CAN I DO TO MAKE IT BETTER

GOALS FOR NEXT WEEK	STEPS ACTION

THOUGHTS & REFLECTIONS

Daily Gratitude Journal

I AM GRATFUL FOR	THE BEST THINGS ABOUT THIS WEEK

ISSUES I HAD AND WHAT CAN I DO TO MAKE IT BETTER

GOALS FOR NEXT WEEK	STEPS ACTION

THOUGHTS & REFLECTIONS

Daily Gratitude Journal

I AM GRATFUL FOR	THE BEST THINGS ABOUT THIS WEEK

ISSUES I HAD AND WHAT CAN I DO TO MAKE IT BETTER

GOALS FOR NEXT WEEK	STEPS ACTION

THOUGHTS & REFLECTIONS

Daily Gratitude Journal

I AM GRATFUL FOR	THE BEST THINGS ABOUT THIS WEEK

ISSUES I HAD AND WHAT CAN I DO TO MAKE IT BETTER

GOALS FOR NEXT WEEK	STEPS ACTION

THOUGHTS & REFLECTIONS

Daily Gratitude Journal

I AM GRATFUL FOR	THE BEST THINGS ABOUT THIS WEEK

ISSUES I HAD AND WHAT CAN I DO TO MAKE IT BETTER

GOALS FOR NEXT WEEK	STEPS ACTION

THOUGHTS & REFLECTIONS

Daily Gratitude Journal

I AM GRATFUL FOR	THE BEST THINGS ABOUT THIS WEEK

ISSUES I HAD AND WHAT CAN I DO TO MAKE IT BETTER

GOALS FOR NEXT WEEK	STEPS ACTION

THOUGHTS & REFLECTIONS

Daily Gratitude Journal

I AM GRATFUL FOR	THE BEST THINGS ABOUT THIS WEEK

ISSUES I HAD AND WHAT CAN I DO TO MAKE IT BETTER

GOALS FOR NEXT WEEK	STEPS ACTION

THOUGHTS & REFLECTIONS

Daily Gratitude Journal

I AM GRATFUL FOR	THE BEST THINGS ABOUT THIS WEEK

ISSUES I HAD AND WHAT CAN I DO TO MAKE IT BETTER

GOALS FOR NEXT WEEK	STEPS ACTION

THOUGHTS & REFLECTIONS

Daily Gratitude Journal

I AM GRATEFUL FOR	THE BEST THINGS ABOUT THIS WEEK

ISSUES I HAD AND WHAT CAN I DO TO MAKE IT BETTER

GOALS FOR NEXT WEEK	STEPS ACTION

THOUGHTS & REFLECTIONS

Daily Gratitude Journal

I AM GRATFUL FOR	THE BEST THINGS ABOUT THIS WEEK

ISSUES I HAD AND WHAT CAN I DO TO MAKE IT BETTER

GOALS FOR NEXT WEEK	STEPS ACTION

THOUGHTS & REFLECTIONS

Daily Gratitude Journal

I AM GRATFUL FOR	THE BEST THINGS ABOUT THIS WEEK

ISSUES I HAD AND WHAT CAN I DO TO MAKE IT BETTER

GOALS FOR NEXT WEEK	STEPS ACTION

THOUGHTS & REFLECTIONS

Daily Gratitude Journal

I AM GRATFUL FOR	THE BEST THINGS ABOUT THIS WEEK

ISSUES I HAD AND WHAT CAN I DO TO MAKE IT BETTER

GOALS FOR NEXT WEEK	STEPS ACTION

THOUGHTS & REFLECTIONS

Daily Gratitude Journal

I AM GRATFUL FOR	THE BEST THINGS ABOUT THIS WEEK

ISSUES I HAD AND WHAT CAN I DO TO MAKE IT BETTER

GOALS FOR NEXT WEEK	STEPS ACTION

THOUGHTS & REFLECTIONS

Daily Gratitude Journal

I AM GRATFUL FOR	THE BEST THINGS ABOUT THIS WEEK

ISSUES I HAD AND WHAT CAN I DO TO MAKE IT BETTER

GOALS FOR NEXT WEEK	STEPS ACTION

THOUGHTS & REFLECTIONS

Daily Gratitude Journal

I AM GRATFUL FOR	THE BEST THINGS ABOUT THIS WEEK

ISSUES I HAD AND WHAT CAN I DO TO MAKE IT BETTER

GOALS FOR NEXT WEEK	STEPS ACTION

THOUGHTS & REFLECTIONS

Daily Gratitude Journal

I AM GRATFUL FOR	THE BEST THINGS ABOUT THIS WEEK

ISSUES I HAD AND WHAT CAN I DO TO MAKE IT BETTER

GOALS FOR NEXT WEEK	STEPS ACTION

THOUGHTS & REFLECTIONS

Daily Gratitude Journal

I AM GRATFUL FOR	THE BEST THINGS ABOUT THIS WEEK

ISSUES I HAD AND WHAT CAN I DO TO MAKE IT BETTER

GOALS FOR NEXT WEEK	STEPS ACTION

THOUGHTS & REFLECTIONS

Daily Gratitude Journal

I AM GRATFUL FOR	THE BEST THINGS ABOUT THIS WEEK

ISSUES I HAD AND WHAT CAN I DO TO MAKE IT BETTER

GOALS FOR NEXT WEEK	STEPS ACTION

THOUGHTS & REFLECTIONS

Daily Gratitude Journal

I AM GRATFUL FOR	THE BEST THINGS ABOUT THIS WEEK

ISSUES I HAD AND WHAT CAN I DO TO MAKE IT BETTER

GOALS FOR NEXT WEEK	STEPS ACTION

THOUGHTS & REFLECTIONS

Daily Gratitude Journal

I AM GRATFUL FOR	THE BEST THINGS ABOUT THIS WEEK

ISSUES I HAD AND WHAT CAN I DO TO MAKE IT BETTER

GOALS FOR NEXT WEEK	STEPS ACTION

THOUGHTS & REFLECTIONS

Daily Gratitude Journal

I AM GRATEFUL FOR	THE BEST THINGS ABOUT THIS WEEK

ISSUES I HAD AND WHAT CAN I DO TO MAKE IT BETTER

GOALS FOR NEXT WEEK	STEPS ACTION

THOUGHTS & REFLECTIONS

Daily Gratitude Journal

I AM GRATFUL FOR	THE BEST THINGS ABOUT THIS WEEK

ISSUES I HAD AND WHAT CAN I DO TO MAKE IT BETTER

___

GOALS FOR NEXT WEEK	STEPS ACTION

THOUGHTS & REFLECTIONS

Daily Gratitude Journal

I AM GRATFUL FOR	THE BEST THINGS ABOUT THIS WEEK

ISSUES I HAD AND WHAT CAN I DO TO MAKE IT BETTER

GOALS FOR NEXT WEEK	STEPS ACTION

THOUGHTS & REFLECTIONS

Daily Gratitude Journal

I AM GRATFUL FOR	THE BEST THINGS ABOUT THIS WEEK

ISSUES I HAD AND WHAT CAN I DO TO MAKE IT BETTER

GOALS FOR NEXT WEEK	STEPS ACTION

THOUGHTS & REFLECTIONS

Daily Gratitude Journal

I AM GRATEFUL FOR	THE BEST THINGS ABOUT THIS WEEK

ISSUES I HAD AND WHAT CAN I DO TO MAKE IT BETTER

GOALS FOR NEXT WEEK	STEPS ACTION

THOUGHTS & REFLECTIONS

Daily Gratitude Journal

I AM GRATFUL FOR	THE BEST THINGS ABOUT THIS WEEK

ISSUES I HAD AND WHAT CAN I DO TO MAKE IT BETTER

GOALS FOR NEXT WEEK	STEPS ACTION

THOUGHTS & REFLECTIONS

Daily Gratitude Journal

I AM GRATFUL FOR	THE BEST THINGS ABOUT THIS WEEK

ISSUES I HAD AND WHAT CAN I DO TO MAKE IT BETTER

GOALS FOR NEXT WEEK	STEPS ACTION

THOUGHTS & REFLECTIONS

Daily Gratitude Journal

| I AM GRATFUL FOR | THE BEST THINGS ABOUT THIS WEEK |
|---|---|//

ISSUES I HAD AND WHAT CAN I DO TO MAKE IT BETTER

GOALS FOR NEXT WEEK	STEPS ACTION

THOUGHTS & REFLECTIONS

Daily Gratitude Journal

I AM GRATFUL FOR	THE BEST THINGS ABOUT THIS WEEK

ISSUES I HAD AND WHAT CAN I DO TO MAKE IT BETTER

GOALS FOR NEXT WEEK	STEPS ACTION

THOUGHTS & REFLECTIONS

Daily Gratitude Journal

I AM GRATFUL FOR	THE BEST THINGS ABOUT THIS WEEK

ISSUES I HAD AND WHAT CAN I DO TO MAKE IT BETTER

GOALS FOR NEXT WEEK	STEPS ACTION

THOUGHTS & REFLECTIONS

Daily Gratitude Journal

I AM GRATFUL FOR	THE BEST THINGS ABOUT THIS WEEK

ISSUES I HAD AND WHAT CAN I DO TO MAKE IT BETTER

GOALS FOR NEXT WEEK	STEPS ACTION

THOUGHTS & REFLECTIONS

Daily Gratitude Journal

I AM GRATFUL FOR	THE BEST THINGS ABOUT THIS WEEK

ISSUES I HAD AND WHAT CAN I DO TO MAKE IT BETTER

GOALS FOR NEXT WEEK	STEPS ACTION

THOUGHTS & REFLECTIONS

Daily Gratitude Journal

I AM GRATFUL FOR	THE BEST THINGS ABOUT THIS WEEK

ISSUES I HAD AND WHAT CAN I DO TO MAKE IT BETTER

GOALS FOR NEXT WEEK	STEPS ACTION

THOUGHTS & REFLECTIONS

Daily Gratitude Journal

I AM GRATFUL FOR	THE BEST THINGS ABOUT THIS WEEK

ISSUES I HAD AND WHAT CAN I DO TO MAKE IT BETTER

GOALS FOR NEXT WEEK	STEPS ACTION

THOUGHTS & REFLECTIONS

Daily Gratitude Journal

I AM GRATFUL FOR	THE BEST THINGS ABOUT THIS WEEK

ISSUES I HAD AND WHAT CAN I DO TO MAKE IT BETTER

GOALS FOR NEXT WEEK	STEPS ACTION

THOUGHTS & REFLECTIONS

Daily Gratitude Journal

I AM GRATFUL FOR	THE BEST THINGS ABOUT THIS WEEK

ISSUES I HAD AND WHAT CAN I DO TO MAKE IT BETTER

GOALS FOR NEXT WEEK	STEPS ACTION

THOUGHTS & REFLECTIONS

Daily Gratitude Journal

I AM GRATEFUL FOR	THE BEST THINGS ABOUT THIS WEEK

ISSUES I HAD AND WHAT CAN I DO TO MAKE IT BETTER

GOALS FOR NEXT WEEK	STEPS ACTION

THOUGHTS & REFLECTIONS

Daily Gratitude Journal

I AM GRATEFUL FOR	THE BEST THINGS ABOUT THIS WEEK

ISSUES I HAD AND WHAT CAN I DO TO MAKE IT BETTER

GOALS FOR NEXT WEEK	STEPS ACTION

THOUGHTS & REFLECTIONS

Daily Gratitude Journal

I AM GRATFUL FOR	THE BEST THINGS ABOUT THIS WEEK

ISSUES I HAD AND WHAT CAN I DO TO MAKE IT BETTER

GOALS FOR NEXT WEEK	STEPS ACTION

THOUGHTS & REFLECTIONS

Daily Gratitude Journal

I AM GRATFUL FOR	THE BEST THINGS ABOUT THIS WEEK

ISSUES I HAD AND WHAT CAN I DO TO MAKE IT BETTER

GOALS FOR NEXT WEEK	STEPS ACTION

THOUGHTS & REFLECTIONS

Daily Gratitude Journal

I AM GRATEFUL FOR	THE BEST THINGS ABOUT THIS WEEK

ISSUES I HAD AND WHAT CAN I DO TO MAKE IT BETTER

GOALS FOR NEXT WEEK	STEPS ACTION

THOUGHTS & REFLECTIONS

Daily Gratitude Journal

I AM GRATFUL FOR	THE BEST THINGS ABOUT THIS WEEK

ISSUES I HAD AND WHAT CAN I DO TO MAKE IT BETTER

GOALS FOR NEXT WEEK	STEPS ACTION

THOUGHTS & REFLECTIONS

Daily Gratitude Journal

I AM GRATFUL FOR	THE BEST THINGS ABOUT THIS WEEK

ISSUES I HAD AND WHAT CAN I DO TO MAKE IT BETTER

GOALS FOR NEXT WEEK	STEPS ACTION

THOUGHTS & REFLECTIONS

Daily Gratitude Journal

I AM GRATFUL FOR	THE BEST THINGS ABOUT THIS WEEK

ISSUES I HAD AND WHAT CAN I DO TO MAKE IT BETTER

GOALS FOR NEXT WEEK	STEPS ACTION

THOUGHTS & REFLECTIONS

Daily Gratitude Journal

I AM GRATEFUL FOR	THE BEST THINGS ABOUT THIS WEEK

ISSUES I HAD AND WHAT CAN I DO TO MAKE IT BETTER

GOALS FOR NEXT WEEK	STEPS ACTION

THOUGHTS & REFLECTIONS

Daily Gratitude Journal

I AM GRATFUL FOR	THE BEST THINGS ABOUT THIS WEEK

ISSUES I HAD AND WHAT CAN I DO TO MAKE IT BETTER

GOALS FOR NEXT WEEK	STEPS ACTION

THOUGHTS & REFLECTIONS

Daily Gratitude Journal

I AM GRATFUL FOR	THE BEST THINGS ABOUT THIS WEEK

ISSUES I HAD AND WHAT CAN I DO TO MAKE IT BETTER

GOALS FOR NEXT WEEK	STEPS ACTION

THOUGHTS & REFLECTIONS

Daily Gratitude Journal

I AM GRATFUL FOR	THE BEST THINGS ABOUT THIS WEEK

ISSUES I HAD AND WHAT CAN I DO TO MAKE IT BETTER

GOALS FOR NEXT WEEK	STEPS ACTION

THOUGHTS & REFLECTIONS

Daily Gratitude Journal

I AM GRATEFUL FOR	THE BEST THINGS ABOUT THIS WEEK

ISSUES I HAD AND WHAT CAN I DO TO MAKE IT BETTER

GOALS FOR NEXT WEEK	STEPS ACTION

THOUGHTS & REFLECTIONS

Daily Gratitude Journal

I AM GRATFUL FOR	THE BEST THINGS ABOUT THIS WEEK

ISSUES I HAD AND WHAT CAN I DO TO MAKE IT BETTER

GOALS FOR NEXT WEEK	STEPS ACTION

THOUGHTS & REFLECTIONS

Daily Gratitude Journal

I AM GRATFUL FOR	THE BEST THINGS ABOUT THIS WEEK

ISSUES I HAD AND WHAT CAN I DO TO MAKE IT BETTER

GOALS FOR NEXT WEEK	STEPS ACTION

THOUGHTS & REFLECTIONS

Daily Gratitude Journal

| I AM GRATFUL FOR | THE BEST THINGS ABOUT THIS WEEK |
|---|---|//

ISSUES I HAD AND WHAT CAN I DO TO MAKE IT BETTER

GOALS FOR NEXT WEEK	STEPS ACTION

THOUGHTS & REFLECTIONS

Daily Gratitude Journal

I AM GRATFUL FOR	THE BEST THINGS ABOUT THIS WEEK

ISSUES I HAD AND WHAT CAN I DO TO MAKE IT BETTER

GOALS FOR NEXT WEEK	STEPS ACTION

THOUGHTS & REFLECTIONS

Daily Gratitude Journal

I AM GRATFUL FOR	THE BEST THINGS ABOUT THIS WEEK

ISSUES I HAD AND WHAT CAN I DO TO MAKE IT BETTER

GOALS FOR NEXT WEEK	STEPS ACTION

THOUGHTS & REFLECTIONS

Daily Gratitude Journal

I AM GRATFUL FOR	THE BEST THINGS ABOUT THIS WEEK

ISSUES I HAD AND WHAT CAN I DO TO MAKE IT BETTER

_____
_____
_____
_____
_____

GOALS FOR NEXT WEEK	STEPS ACTION

THOUGHTS & REFLECTIONS

_____
_____
_____
_____
_____

Daily Gratitude Journal

I AM GRATFUL FOR	THE BEST THINGS ABOUT THIS WEEK

ISSUES I HAD AND WHAT CAN I DO TO MAKE IT BETTER

GOALS FOR NEXT WEEK	STEPS ACTION

THOUGHTS & REFLECTIONS

Daily Gratitude Journal

I AM GRATEFUL FOR	THE BEST THINGS ABOUT THIS WEEK

ISSUES I HAD AND WHAT CAN I DO TO MAKE IT BETTER

GOALS FOR NEXT WEEK	STEPS ACTION

THOUGHTS & REFLECTIONS

Daily Gratitude Journal

I AM GRATFUL FOR	THE BEST THINGS ABOUT THIS WEEK

ISSUES I HAD AND WHAT CAN I DO TO MAKE IT BETTER

GOALS FOR NEXT WEEK	STEPS ACTION

THOUGHTS & REFLECTIONS

Daily Gratitude Journal

I AM GRATFUL FOR	THE BEST THINGS ABOUT THIS WEEK

ISSUES I HAD AND WHAT CAN I DO TO MAKE IT BETTER

GOALS FOR NEXT WEEK	STEPS ACTION

THOUGHTS & REFLECTIONS

Daily Gratitude Journal

I AM GRATFUL FOR	THE BEST THINGS ABOUT THIS WEEK

ISSUES I HAD AND WHAT CAN I DO TO MAKE IT BETTER

GOALS FOR NEXT WEEK	STEPS ACTION

THOUGHTS & REFLECTIONS

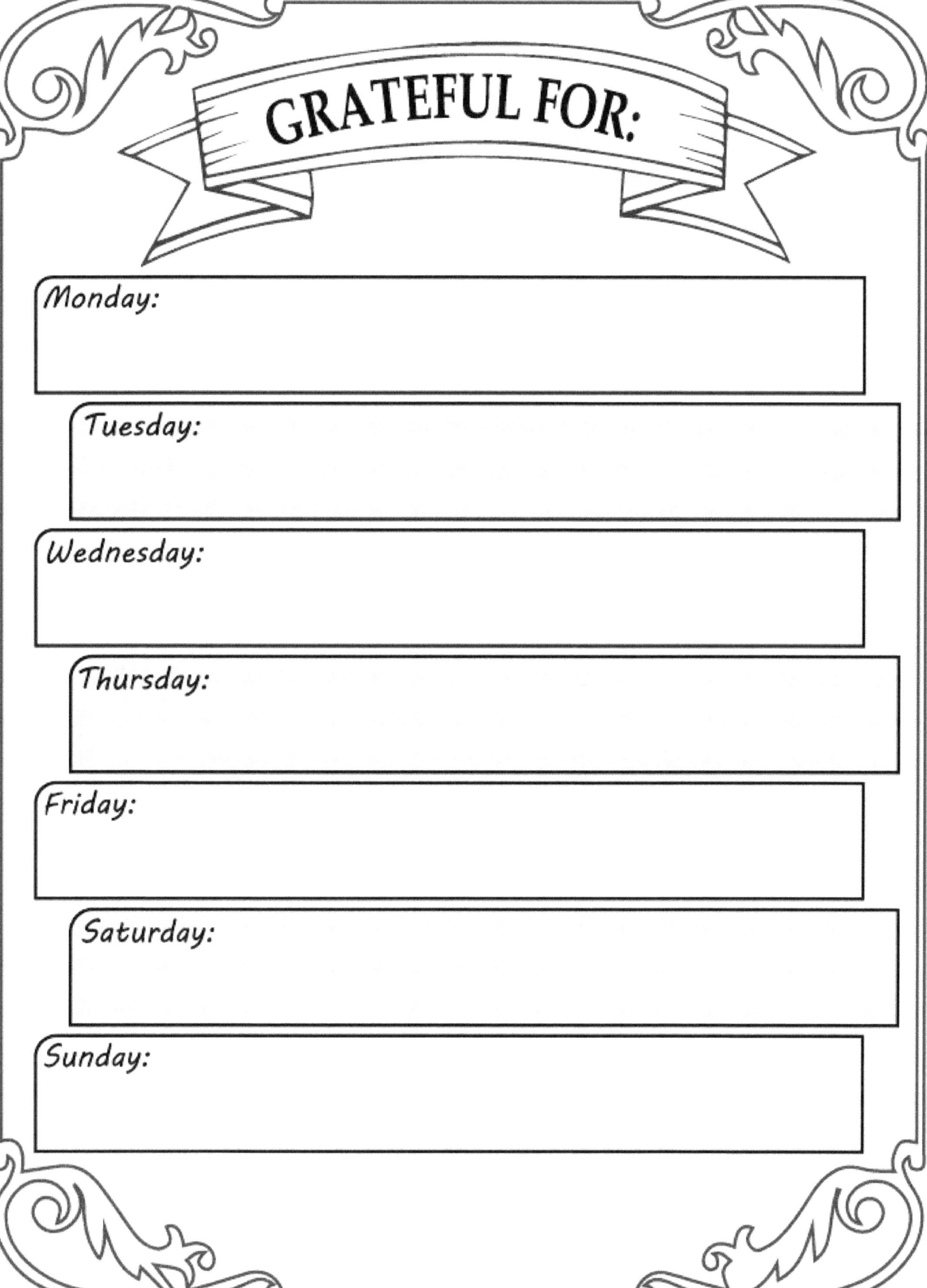

Thank You

Dear
_____
_____
_____
_____
_____
_____
_____
_____

_____
_____
_____

You don't actually have to send the letter

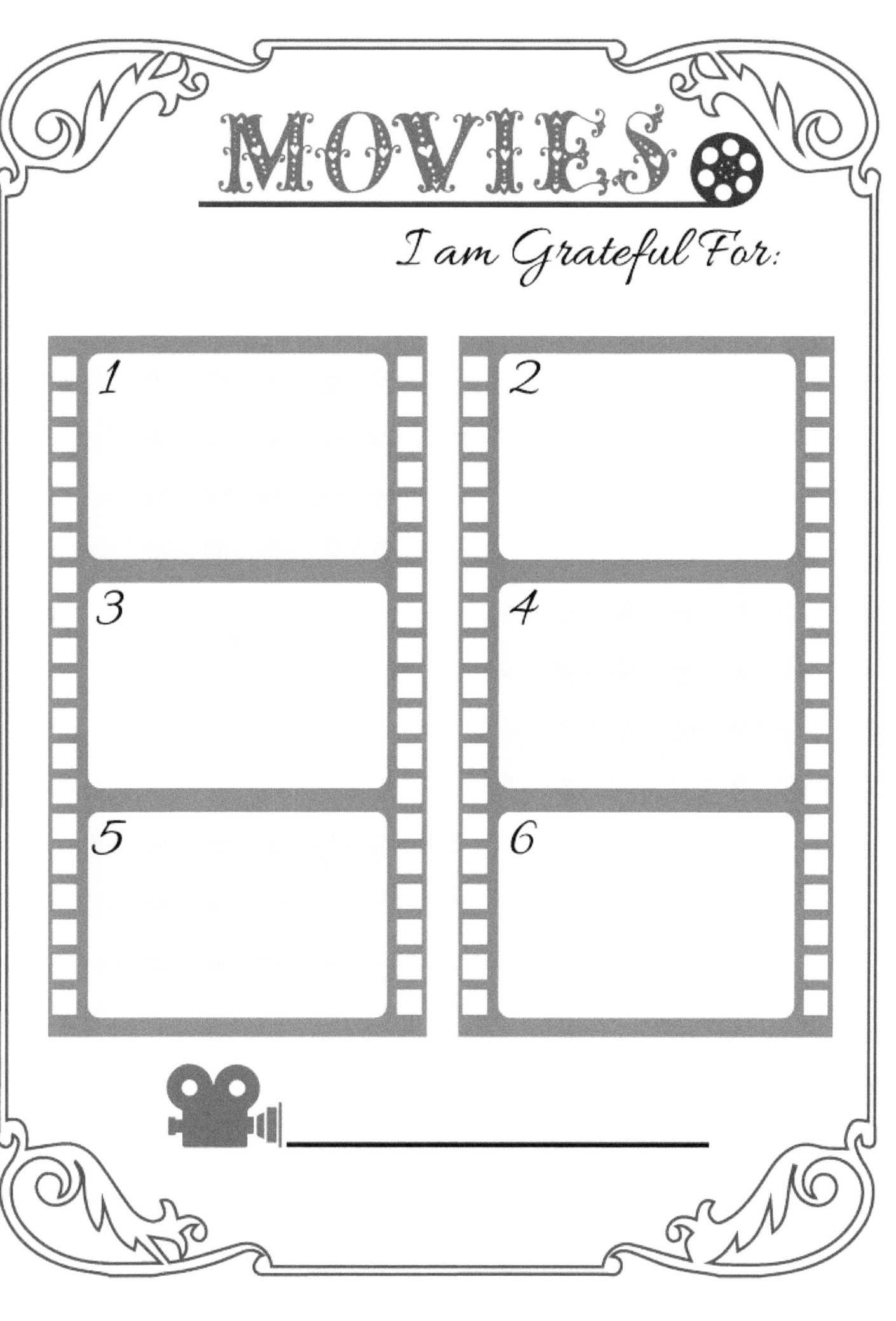

The activities that make me happy:

_____
_____
_____
_____

I will try to do them more often by:

_____
_____
_____
_____

Gratitude Prompts

Please use the following prompts to utilize when requiring prompts

22. What is your biggest accomplishment?
23. Do you have a family tradition that you enjoy?
24. What are your good qualities?
25. What are your hobbies?
26. Is there anything that makes your life better?
27. What movie did you like?
28. What books did you enjoy?
29. Who made you smile?
30. Write about a nice thing somebody said to you.
31. Who do you enjoy spending time with?
32. What songs do you love?
33. Where is the best place you visited and what do you like about it?
34. What have you learned?
35. Has anyone shown you kindness recently?
36. What do you love about your home?
37. What do you love about your country?
38. Describe the last gift you received. Who gave it to you?

Gratitude Prompts

Please use the following prompts to utilize when requiring prompts

22. What is your biggest accomplishment?
23. Do you have a family tradition that you enjoy?
24. What are your good qualities?
25. What are your hobbies?
26. Is there anything that makes your life better?
27. What movie did you like?
28. What books did you enjoy?
29. Who made you smile?
30. Write about a nice thing somebody said to you.
31. Who do you enjoy spending time with?
32. What songs do you love?
33. Where is the best place you visited and what do you like about it?
34. What have you learned?
35. Has anyone shown you kindness recently?
36. What do you love about your home?
37. What do you love about your country?
38. Describe the last gift you received. Who gave it to you?

Gratitude Prompts

39. What do you like about yourself?
40. What do you like about your job?
41. In what way is your life better today than it was a year ago or ten years ago?
42. What is the nicest thing that someone did for you?
43. Describe one of your best days.
44. What do you enjoy doing after work?
45. What do you enjoy doing as you get home?
46. Describe a bad experience that made you stronger.
47. What do you have today that you didn't have as a child?
48. Describe a difficulty that you have overcome.
49. What would you take to a desert island?
50. What was the last thing that made you laugh?
51. What is your favorite animal?
52. What cheers you up when you are feeling sad?
53. What do you enjoy about your daily routine?
54. Describe your last vacation?
55. What have you accomplished?

Let's Connect

Newsletter

Sign up for our monthly newsletter and receive up to date information on new products and information to assist and support you in your continued personal growth and so much more.

https://www.moreenjordan.com

and go to sign up for Newsletter

Social Media Facebook:

@ AspiringLifeChange Counseling & Consulting

Website

https://www.moreenjordan.com

Wrapping Up!

Self care is extremely important. You can give more, and you can become more connected with yourself. You will be able to handle stress better and you can become more productive in your day and relationships. These are just a few of the benefits of effective self care. It is important to re-evaluation your self care levels and needs throughout your life. You can take the self care quiz whenever you feel there has been life changes and your need to re-evaluate if you are still addressing caring well for yourself

You can do this.
You deserve this!
Self care is not selfish!

www.ingramcontent.com/pod-product-compliance
Lightning Source LLC
Chambersburg PA
CBHW081509080526
44589CB00017B/2706